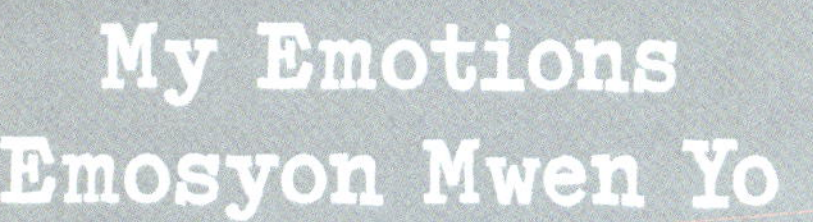

BORED
RAZ

A Crabtree Roots Book
Yon Liv Crabtree Rasin

AMY CULLIFORD
JEAN-PIERRE GASTON

Crabtree Publishing
crabtreebooks.com

School-to-Home Support for Caregivers and Teachers

This book helps children grow by letting them practice reading. Here are a few guiding questions to help the reader with building his or her comprehension skills. Possible answers appear here in red.

Before Reading:

- What do I think this book is about?
  - *This book is about feeling bored.*
  - *This book is about what feeling bored looks or feels like.*

- What do I want to learn about this topic?
  - *I want to learn what makes people feel bored.*
  - *I want to learn what feeling bored looks like.*

During Reading:

- I wonder why...
  - *I wonder why we yawn when we are bored.*
  - *I wonder what we can do when we are bored.*

- What have I learned so far?
  - *I have learned that you can read if you are bored.*
  - *I have learned that you can play a game if you are bored.*

After Reading:

- What details did I learn about this topic?
  - *I have learned that it is okay to feel bored.*
  - *I have learned that there are many things you can do when you feel bored.*

- Read the book again and look for the vocabulary words.
  - *I see the word* ***rains*** *on page 4 and the word* ***yawn*** *on page 6. The other vocabulary words are found on page 14.*

I am **bored**.

Mwen **raz**.

I am bored when it **rains**.

Mwen raz lè **lapli** tonbe.

I **yawn** when I am bored.

Mwen **baye** lè mwen raz.

I am bored in the **car**.

Mwen raz nan **machin** nan.

I **read** when I am bored.

Mwen **li** yon liv lè mwen raz.

I play a **game** when I am bored.

Mwen jwe yon **jwèt** lè mwen raz.

When do you feel bored?

Kilè ou santi ou raz?

Words to Know
Palabras para conocer

bored
raz

car
machin

game
jwèt

rains
lapli

read
li

yawn
baye

40 Words

I am **bored**.

I am bored when it **rains**.

I **yawn** when I am bored.

I am bored in the **car**.

I **read** when I am bored.

I play a **game** when I am bored.

When do you feel bored?

36 mo

Mwen **raz**?

Mwen raz lè **lapli** tonbe.

Mwen **baye** lè mwen raz.

Mwen raz nan **machin** nan.

Mwen **li** yon liv lè mwen raz.

Mwen jwe yon **jwèt** lè mwen raz.

Kilè ou santi ou raz?

My Emotions

BORED

Emosyon Mwen Yo

RAZ

Written by: Amy Culliford

Designed by: Rhea Wallace

Series Development: James Earley

Proofreader: Ellen Rodger

Educational Consultant: Marie Lemke M.Ed.

Photographs:
Shutterstock: Juan Pablo Gonzaález: cover; diplomedia: p. 1; Syda Productions: p. 3, 14; GOLFX: p. 5, 14; airdone: p. 7, 14; Leszek Glasner: p. 8-9, 14; Zurijeta: p. 10, 14; Motortion Films: p. 11, 14; fizkes: p. 13

Crabtree Publishing

crabtreebooks.com 800-387-7650

Printed in Canada/042023/CPC20230419

Published in Canada
Crabtree Publishing
616 Welland Ave.
St. Catharines, Ontario
L2M 5V6

Published in the United States
Crabtree Publishing
347 Fifth Avenue,
Suite 1402-145
New York, NY, 10016

Library and Archives Canada Cataloguing in Publication
Available at the Library and Archives Canada

Library of Congress Cataloging-in-Publication Data
Available at the Library of Congress

Paperback: 9781039624566
Ebook: 9781039625402
Epub: 9781039624986